Praise for Your Family Legacy

"Once you decide where you want to go financially, Mike's book (and his advice) is the GPS that gets you to your destination."

— Don Beal, retired &
Janet Beal, Second Generation, Tarco Steel

Fabulous concepts on how to pass your family business, values and legacy on to the "text" generation! Compelling concepts – my favorite: Success is not determined by your IQ, but rather your I-cubed (I^3)!

— Sallie "Alligator Sallie" Meshell,
co-author *Jump Start Your Success*

"An easy read yet thought-provoking. I was lost in thought between pages as I tried to apply his ideas to my family. Michael presents many good ideas and leaves you with the desire and resources to learn more. I'll definitely look into those resources!"

— Nancy Shepard, Retired IBM Executive

"Michael Palumbos' book *Your Family Legacy* is a home run! He has broken down a complex topic into bite-size pieces. We can easily use his steps to create our own personal family legacy that will last for many generations. Give this gift to your unborn heirs, you'll be glad you did!"

— Gary Barnes, author *Into the Night* and creator of
On Purpose Results

"An easy read, that packs a punch"

— John J. Cogan, Vantage Benefits Group

"A quick, fun read. It really got me thinking about legacy and what we truly leave behind."

— Phil Rubenstein, President
United Radio, Third Generation Family Business

"Too often the estate plan becomes a collection of documents which the client often doesn't understand. It should start with a collection of thoughts about the family without regard to tax. Only after that can a document be considered. This book clearly addresses the process for developing thoughts. Great starting point."

— Michael E. O'Connor, Esq., author of Estate Planning:
Beyond the Basics. Partner, DeLaney & O'Connor, LLP

"A great read to help generate ideas. I will use it with our Next Generation Roundtable as they prepare to become leaders."

— Donna Herlihy, President
New York Family Business Center

"Michael identifies the tremendous need for values planning in conjunction with financial planning. The most important thing we can provide our children, our grandchidren and our great grandchildren is the ability to carry forward what we value as a family. The financial resources we accumulate and distribute for their use are simply a tool to further the family mission. The most solid of families share common values over financial resources. Planning the finances for a family is simply not enough in today's world."

— John Enright, Owner Custom Wealth Architects

Your Family
LEGACY

32 ways to preserve your family's 'wealth' for generations

MICHAEL PALUMBOS

Editors:
Elizabeth MacBride
527 Putnam Place
Alexandria, Va. 22302
703-548-3087
elizabeth.macbride5@gmail.com

Cathy Godlewski
Write Mind
P.O. Box 593
Victor, NY 14564
585.393.1451
cathy@write-mind.com
www.write-mind.com

Cover and Interior Design:
Dawn Teagarden
dawn@teagardendesigns.com

I'd like to dedicate this book to my family. Each and everyone of you has impacted me and pushed me to be a better husband, father, son, grandson, brother, brother-in-law, nephew, cousin and uncle.

I love you all and am proud to call you my family.

Contents

Preface

Economists tell us that the family business is the backbone of America. How big is that backbone? Just for a baseline, **Google** "Family Owned Businesses" and you get a fairly respectable 6 million hits. But by comparison, **Google** "All Businesses in America" and 1.2 billion hits pop up. Now that doesn't prove anything but it is interesting that the family business, so crucial to the success of America, doesn't show as much on the internet as other business ventures.

Looking more closely at a family business you'll often find a Mom and Dad who worked 18 hours a day for years establishing a business in the hopes of permitting a better life for themselves and their family. Their children grow up in an environment where their family life is defined by the family business. Soccer games and school concerts often fall victim to delivery deadlines or client meetings. The children learn the business and often find they are more at home working than they are at play. Some of the most successful companies in America started this way.

It has been my privilege to work in a family business of my own which spans five decades. Our mission is to help family owned companies navigate the business and family challenges in their own lives. In a competitive world, regulated by ever changing tax laws, complicated by family dynamics, all in addition to the normal pressures of business; collecting as much information as you can and surrounding yourself with a team of trusted advisors is the best advice a family business owner can get.

No one approach or technique can assure that the desire to work on building a legacy will work, but one thing is certain. In the absence of a plan to control our future, it will certainly control us. Gathered in these pages are some superb ideas to start or continue the thinking process as you examine your own family and what your legacy will be.

By way of example I offer a little background on our family and our family business just as a way to say we are in the very same process of examining our family legacy as we encourage you to pursue.

In 1999 our entire family began a tradition that lives until today and our collective plans call for this annual event to continue on into the future. As you surely know yourself the logistical challenge of bringing 23 humans together for a one week common event is massive. Palumbos Family Vacation has been an opportunity to see each other and build or renew the bonds of love in the family. For some of our family it is the only vacation they get all year.

In our family business, rooted in the financial service industry, incentive travel has been a motivation technique that our family has benefited from for years. Working for years without rest, as many business owners do, we have always had the benefit of an industry that has valued stopping to celebrate accomplishment and reward good results.

Having learned this first hand in the business world, it was an easy transition to take the same concept of relaxation and reward to the family. In our early years our gatherings were in our home and the entertainment was being with each other peppered in with a trip to the local beach.

As the family grew and as resources permitted we have enjoyed some trips away to exotic locales and memorable sights but the common thread has always been the family together celebrating our life accomplishments and enjoying the rewards of hard work.

As you make your way through this book, do your best to take away some ideas that you can bring to your own family and your business. No one can guarantee your success but yourself.

I wish you well!

Martin "Marty" Palumbos
First Generation Business Owner
& more importantly, Michael's father

Foreword

A few years ago I was privileged to represent a man who was the son of an immigrant painter. While he had grown up with very little in the way of financial wealth, he was no stranger to hard work. By the time he was 21, he had saved enough from painting houses and apartments to begin investing in real estate. Thirty years later he had amassed a fortune in commercial real estate and founded a significant financial services firm.

One day I journeyed to his home, a mansion he had restored to the magnificence it had enjoyed more than a century earlier when its first owner had built it on a summit overlooking . After touring the home, I began to ask him a series of reflective questions. His answer to one of those questions harmonizes extremely well with the wisdom you will find in *Your Family Legacy.*

I asked this entrepreneur if there was a secret formula he had discovered for creating financial wealth to which he replied, without hesitation: "If you took all of my wealth away tomorrow, within a year I'd be a millionaire again."

There was no arrogance in his statement. But the absolute confidence in his voice led me to inquire deeper. He explained, "The most difficult million dollars any one ever makes is their first million. After you have discovered what it takes in terms of energy, vision, wise choices and persistence to make that first million, you have the recipe for wealth. Take it all away but leave me with that recipe, and I will find a way within a year to start building another fortune."

As I left this self-made millionaire I wondered what it would take for him to be able to pass that recipe along to his family. I have found that while many will make millions only a few discover the secrets for passing the formula for building and preserving that financial fortune to their heirs. Even fewer begin and complete the process Michael Palumbos suggests.

Is it more difficult to leave a positive and sustainable legacy than it is to accumulate our first million dollars? Pondering that question can serve as the knob to the door of insight. One important insight I have gained from *Your Family Legacy* is the formula Mr. Palumbos developed to help families redefine their concept of success. He calls it the I^3 formula. And, Michael's Lifestyle and Legacy Planning Pyramid is a marvelously effective roadmap to help you live and leave a lasting legacy.

But we should not be fooled by the simplicity of Mr. Palumbos' suggestions. It takes significant vision, along with time and energy, to reach the pinnacle of his Legacy Planning Pyramid.

A clear dream or vision of what we would like our legacy to be is one of the keys I believe we need to utilize in harnessing the opportunity Michael has given us with this book. In offering his professional wisdom Michael is living his own legacy because his highest professional calling is to "passionately energize others to create innovative visions that inspire action."

In early 2008 I had the opportunity to address 20 self-made men, all of whom were worth at least $250 million and several of whom had become billionaires. Before I started my presentation I asked them this question: "(h)ow many of you had a dream which fueled and propelled you along the path you took to reach your ultimate financial success?" Eighteen of the twenty men raised their hands. I then turned to the two men who disavowed having a dream which they had followed to create their fortunes. After further exchanges, it became apparent that each of them didn't feel they had a dream but both had methodically and consistently set short-term and long-term goals which were keys to their success. Was it just a remarkable coincidence that each of these 20 individuals had either been inspired and sustained by a dream or had used persistent goal-setting in their climb to financial success? These words from James Allen provide the answer:

> *"The greatest achievement was at first and for a time a **dream**. The oak sleeps in the acorn, the bird waits in the egg, and in the highest vision of the soul a waking angel stirs. **Dreams are the seedlings of realities.**"*

I am convinced that a dream and then a persistent plan of action are as important when it comes to the important work of leaving a positive and sustainable legacy as they are to the business of creating financial wealth.

We have to work our dreams. That requires time, energy and persistence. It may in fact be much easier to pass on financial wealth than it is the formula for creating and preserving that wealth. But please do not be discouraged by the magnitude of the effort required to both live and leave a legacy. In *Your Family Legacy* Michael points out there are really only three things we can pass on to our heirs: our money, our values and our knowledge. Then he shares this powerful question with us:

> *"If you could only pass two of the three mentioned assets to your heirs, which two would you pick?"*

I strongly suspect as you ponder that question you will feel just how important the work of passing on our values and wisdom is. I encourage you to use *Your Family Legacy* to more clearly define the dream for your personal and family legacy and to purposefully put into motion the simple but effective steps Michael has shared with us.

Nothing we do in our quest to live and leave a legacy is wasted effort. From what may at first appear to be very small steps will come marvelous results. And your family will always be grateful you found the time to read and incorporate ' practical wisdom into your legacy planning.

John "JohnA"Warnick
Founder of The Purposeful Planning Institute

Author's Note

The goal of this book is to help ensure that your family does not fall prey to the "shirtsleeves-to-shirtsleeves in three generations" paradigm that happens to 90 percent of families. Based on research by Roy Williams and Vic Pressier, of the Institute for Preparing Heirs, there is a 70 percent failure rate in passing a family's wealth from generation to generation. That means that by the third generation, family wealth disappears 90 percent of the time. In other words, out of 100 families only 10 will retain their family wealth by the third generation.

This happens for many varied reasons, but it's generally because the second and third generations are not prepared to deal with the wealth. The first generation, whose members worked so hard to accumulate and grow the wealth, did not prepare future generations for its distribution and transfer.

Today, only 7 percent of Americans reach a household net worth (excluding their primary residence) of over $1 million. If you have reached this mile marker, congratulations! ***You obviously <u>think differently</u> than 93 percent of America <u>about acquiring wealth</u>.*** My hope is that I can help you to think differently about preparing your heirs for the distribution and transfer of your accumulated wealth.

I have been working with families and their advisors personally for more than 10 years and my father has been working with families for well over 30 years.

My father taught me something about learning from books, seminars and coaches. He said that if you can walk away from any teacher, book, seminar and/or coach having learned one new thing or be reminded of something you knew but had forgotten, then you have received an invaluable gift. Knowledge once gained may be used again and again.

My question as I thought about writing a book was, "What have we learned and how can we share that knowledge with others?"

At the most basic level, the idea contained in this book is that there can never be enough communication. High level, thought-filled communication is the foundation of trusting relationships within the family and with your advisors. Communication leads to collaboration; collaboration leads to new ideas and better preparation for the impending wealth transfer to the next generation.

When trusting family members collaborate with their trusted advisors, the results can be staggering. Finally, when the family-trusted advisors collaborate with each other, the planning challenges (problems) of the family dissipate.

The French philosopher Voltaire wrote,

"No problem can withstand
the assault of sustained thinking."

We believe a collaborative group of advisors and families working on the challenge of passing down your family's wealth will develop a vision that will hold up for generations.

You do not have to agree with my thinking, but I hope this book will make you pause and ponder about the dynamics within your family. My greatest desire is that one idea from this book becomes a valuable gift for your family.

I look forward to hearing from you and how this little book started a big conversation that became a positive event in your family.

To Your Family Legacy!

Michael Palumbos
200 Meridian Centre
Suite 150
Rochester, NY 14618
(585) 350-7273
info@MichaelPalumbos.com
www.MichaelPalumbos.com

Introduction:
The I³ Formula

Money is the currency by which everybody measures you, but I believe that those families who see income and wealth as only one part of a successful life are more likely to transmit their values over time and be able to successfully pass their wealth down.

In my work with families and advisors over the past 10 years, I have developed a formula — I³ — to help families redefine their concept of success.

The I³ Formula

$$I^3 = \text{Influence x Impact x Income}$$

The I³ formula is a way to think about success in life.

Individuals who have a lot of impact, influence and income are probably already living out their dreams and passions. Families that are helping their members achieve impact, influence and income have an outstanding chance of passing on their values and wealth to the next generation.

I believe that it's natural for us as human beings to want to excel, help others and to succeed.

The greater the influence, the impact and the income a person has throughout his or her life, the more successful s/he feels, and the more s/he has the ability to contribute — to family, friends, the community and society as a whole.

I define the variables this way:

- *Influence*: Your effect on the people around you, especially on your family

- *Impact*: The change you help bring about in the world

- *Income*: The amount of monetary or other rewards that you gather over time

I use the I^3 formula as an incredibly subjective discussion point within a family meeting. When a value from 1 to 10 is assigned for each part of the formula and then multiplied together, we get a score. Sometimes, we compare the same score over the years to see how we're doing.

This could be done both for individuals and the family as a whole.

For example:

$I^3 =$ Influence x Impact x Income

$I^3 = 3$ x 5 x 8

$I^3 = 120$

Or:

$I^3 =$ Influence x Impact x Income

$I^3 = 7$ x 7 x 5

$I^3 = 245$

This framework is designed to be subjective and to be a starting point for a conversation. What is considered a 10 for one family may be lower or higher for another. There is no right or wrong. The fact that you are having the discussion at all is what's important. You're beginning to tackle these sorts of questions: "Are we as individuals within the larger family system living out our dreams and passions? Is the family working to help each individual reach his or her goals?"

The formula does not distinguish between right and wrong, good deeds or bad. Bernie Madoff most certainly lived his life I³. He had a huge impact, was very influential and made tons of income. He was also a crook. On the other hand Bill and Melinda Gates definitely live I³ and they have had a tremendously positive impact on the world. We just picked two very easy situations where I³ was easy to distinguish but what about the story of Oseola McCarty?

Ms. McCarty spent almost her entire life doing laundry for others. She lived simply and happily and in 1995 she gave a gift of approximately $150,000 (60 percent of her life savings) to the University of Southern Mississippi (USM) in order to create a scholarship fund for deserving students in need of financial assistance. Her thinking was that she could help provide a scholarship for black students to attend a college that years ago didn't even admit blacks. The full story is available at http://www.usm.edu/pr/oola1.htm.

What would Ms. McCarty's I³ score be? What a great question for your family to think about.

When we are speaking about income in the formula it does not have to be measured in dollars and cents. I believe we can receive non-monetary items such as, knowledge, spiritual, confidence, trust, happiness, self-esteem and humility to name just a few. King Duncan wrote about how Mother Theresa exemplified this in his book *The Amazing Law of Influence*.

King wrote, "There is a great story surrounding the opening of her AIDS center in New York. While visiting in Sing Sing prison in upstate New York, she found four inmates suffering from AIDS. Without hesitation she went to Mayor Koch's office at City Hall in New York City and asked him to telephone Governor Cuomo on her behalf. She told the governor about the four prisoners and asked him to release them so she could begin her AIDS center.

"The governor replied that they had forty-three cases of AIDS in the state prison system and that he would release them all to her. She said four was enough to begin. Then she asked the governor for the state to provide a building to house her new center. Cuomo agreed.

"Then she turned to Mayor Koch and asked him to clear some permits to them to get the center underway immediately. The mayor shook his head back and forth and said, 'As long as you don't make me wash the floors.' "

You see here a woman without any financial income, but she was paid with spiritual and emotional income for the influence that she had with Governor Cuomo and Mayor Koch. The impact that she had didn't stop there; she opened hundreds of AIDS hospices in the United States and around the world.

So, yes, there is a formula, but it's not so simple or cut and dry. It's a way to measure whether you and the members of your family are living your passion.

SECTION I:
Your Family Wealth

How
"Right Planning"
will increase
your I^3 score and
peace of mind

"No problem can be solved from the same level of consciousness that created it."

— Albert Einstein

"Wealth is the ability to fully experience life."

— Henry David Thoreau

"We do not act rightly because we have virtue or excellence, but we rather have those because we have acted rightly."

— Aristotle

"Good fortune is what happens when opportunity meets with planning."

—Thomas Edison

1

Advice From A "Secret Millionaire"

In February of 2011, I hired James Malinchak, ABC's "Secret Millionaire," as my business coach. Seven months later this book was ready to be published. My coach saw things that I had overlooked. James taught me that "working hard and working smart were great but it's working right that makes all the difference."

Allow me to illustrate. You planned hard to save and accumulate everything that you have today. You planned smart by doing things such as diversifying your investments, spending wisely, watching the investment fees you paid, and you purchased insurance to cover any potential shortfalls.

Planning right means that you have your planning audited and tested every year by a specialist (a coach) who is able to objectively look at your family's entire situation. This review spans your financial independence, risk management, estate and legacy, business and benefits, as well as, your investments and tax situation.

We are faced with sky rocketing healthcare costs, mountainous government spending and turbulent stock markets. This is the new "norm" and it will continue for years to come. Annual stress testing of your financial plan will allow you to make decisions and course corrections before it is too late. This will keep you "planning right," as well as planning smart and hard.

2

Recognize The Three Assets

We all have three assets that we have the ability to pass to our heirs: our money, our values and our knowledge. I believe that at the core everything can be placed into one of these three buckets. I know that good health is an incredible asset but it's not an asset that you can pass along (or fully control).

In my work with families, one of my favorite questions to ask is, "If you could only pass two of the three mentioned assets to your heirs, which two would you pick?"

The number one answer is a family's values and knowledge. I think most people would agree that the reasons are almost always the same. If our heirs have our values and knowledge and the money is gone they will have the ability to recreate the wealth.

The next question becomes, "What are you doing as a family to actively capture, catalog and ensure that the values and knowledge of your family are passed along for generations?"

Two things can get in the way of people actively working on their family; time and money. I believe that we all have the best of intentions but we have limited time and I think families are asked to do more and more every year. Families today are stretched in a million directions and society seems to continuously add to the list of things we "must" do for both parents and children (such as start travel sports by kindergarten or get left behind, dance lessons, language classes, update Facebook, LinkedIn and Twitter, don't forget graduations from preschool, kindergarten, 5th, 8th and high school... etc.). If we do not set aside time we will continue to grasp at the "hope" that our children will obtain all that they need. Like a plant starved of water, our children will wilt without the <u>proper attention</u>.

Russ Alan Prince & Associates Inc. conducted a survey in which they asked families with a net worth of $1 to $10 million whether they were concerned about losing their assets. It should not come as a shock to you that 9 out of 10 were "very concerned." What was revealing was that this survey was done in 2005, before the market crash in 2008. I am certain that 100 percent of those families are concerned today and that many families with much higher net worths are concerned as well.

I tell you this because I know how important it is to feel financially independent. More importantly, we need to know with a high degree of certainty that we will be able to maintain our desired lifestyle even when a few unexpected occurrences get thrown at us over the years. All of us need to know that we can maintain our lifestyle before we are able to focus on anyone else, including our children.

3

The Lifestyle And Legacy Planning Pyramid

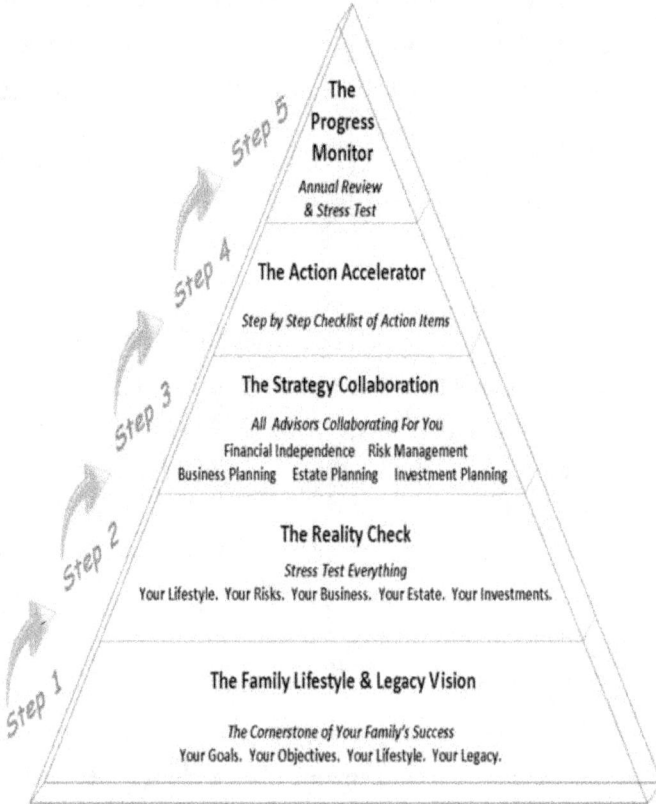

Step 5

The Progress Monitor

Annual Review & Stress Test

Step 4

The Action Accelerator

Step by Step Checklist of Action Items

Step 3

The Strategy Collaboration

All Advisors Collaborating For You

Financial Independence   Risk Management
Business Planning   Estate Planning   Investment Planning

Step 2

The Reality Check

Stress Test Everything
Your Lifestyle. Your Risks. Your Business. Your Estate. Your Investments.

Step 1

The Family Lifestyle & Legacy Vision

The Cornerstone of Your Family's Success
Your Goals. Your Objectives. Your Lifestyle. Your Legacy.

4

Consider These Family-Focused Decisions

When contemplating decisions that affect your family, including financial planning and investment decisions, consider each of these key areas:

- **Vision** – Does this help or detract from our purpose?

- **Collaboration** – Are we working as a team or as individuals?

- **Family Members** – Are we growing our human and intellectual capital?

- **Financial and Social Assets** – Are we investing in the future or spending?

Inevitably, at any given time you will have more focus on one of these four areas than the others. The goal is to consistently remind the family that all four decisions need attention in order to make a big difference over the long term.

5

Find The Right Team To Help You Shape Your Strategy

As a wealth advisor, I know there is no shortage of ideas available on financial planning and investing – different styles, different theories and different planning strategies. You need to create a plan and work with advisors who feel right for you and your family.

Why would someone go through life without a fully stress-tested financial plan? There are three reasons I have witnessed:

1) Some people do not feel the need to plan or feel they are too young.

2) Others do not feel that they can afford the time and/or money to plan.

3) More often it is because they have yet to find an advisor they feel can take their planning to the next level and/or has their family's best interest at heart.

I am certain that if you are taking the time to read this book that you feel the need. Good investments have long-term positive returns attached to them and so will good planning.

If you have put off creating a plan because of the cost, I'd say to you that planning is never a cost, it's always an investment. You would never build a house without blueprint plans or run a business without an emergency plan. Few couples would get married without planning the big day. Proper planning is what allows us to keep our wits about us when things go wrong, and they will.

It is costing you and your family more money by not doing the proper planning than to invest and have it done right. This might mean you have yet to find advisors that you fully trust. You wouldn't do your own heart surgery; you would call a specialist, so why would you consider doing your own planning, personal or business?

If you have yet to create a plan because you haven't met advisors you feel comfortable with, look at the articles available on my web site, www.MichaelPalumbos.com. These articles will show you things to look for in a true specialist, a real wealth advisor.

Most families will have a financial advisor that also manages the investments. The theory is that one advisor or advisor team will better coordinate all of the aspects of the plan (an old mentor of mine used to say anything with two heads was a freak...someone has to lead). The investments may need to be set up a certain way in order to make the overall plan work.

Having said that...the financial advisor may help the family find money managers that fit well with the investment portion of the financial plan. They don't create the plan; instead they manage the money in accordance with their mandate.

A good financial advisor or wealth manager will provide checks and balances between the wealth manager and the family.

Your wealth advisor should help you create a financial plan and set an investment strategy. They may manage the investments themselves, or they might help you find a good money manager.

In addition to advisors to help with your financial plan and manage money, families might also need some or all of the following services: a CPA, an estate/tax planning attorney, a business attorney and a family wealth coach or therapist.

In the end each family is different and will have different needs. The most important thing is that the advisors collaborate for the good of the family.

Another important thing to keep in mind is that the advisors who helped you acquire and manage your wealth may not be the right people to guide you on its transfer. Think about it in the same way that you wouldn't have that heart surgeon operate on your knee. You need to think about each stage of your wealth and gauge whether each advisor is properly suited to handle the new task at hand.

When choosing advisors, it's essential that you find specialists who work well together, with your family, and with you and your spouse. There is no one-size-fits-all plan, and one planning technique won't work for everyone. Just because your golf buddy utilized a planning technique that he feels worked wonders for his tax situation, that doesn't mean that it is the right solution for your family. There is such a plethora of information available that you'll probably have multiple options, all with pros and cons. You need people who will work together to create a plan that is customized to fit your family's lifestyle and legacy vision.

Make sure you are comfortable with your decisions. Ensure that your team of advisors is stocked with great listeners and that they *hear* exactly what you and your family desire.

Michael Palumbos

6

Create A Plan And Triple Test It

There are three common worries that individuals have when they retire, other than the obvious worry about maintaining one's health.

1) Will I run out of assets?

2) Will there be enough income for both my spouse and I?

3) Will my kids and grandchildren be alright?

In order to do any planning for your heirs, first ensure that you and your spouse are comfortable with any retirement/lifestyle plan that you have put together. If you are not comfortable then go back and have the figures tested again. Have them tested until you are 100 percent satisfied and confident with your future lifestyle.

There are three tests that I have found to be very helpful in satisfying the question, "Are we going to be okay?"

1) **The 4 Percent Rule:** This has been tested through the years and has held up extremely well over time. Simply put, a person can spend 4 percent of the value of their portfolio the first year of their retirement and increase it for inflation annually. A person with a $1 million portfolio will be able to spend $40,000 in year one of retirement. This figure doesn't include any pension, social security or other forms of income.

2) **Monte Carlo Analysis:** This is a mathematical algorithm performed by a computer that measures risk during retirement.

In other words, programmed with decades of stock market data a probable outcome for retirement can be shown as a percentage of possible success. The more times the simulation is run, the more accurate the output. I like to see between 500 to 1,000 tests run.

Remember flipping a coin and recording heads or tails in grammar school? That's Monte Carlo analysis or probability. If we only flipped the coin a handful of times your percentage of heads to tails may be skewed but when the coin is flipped numerous times, the outcome would be 50 percent heads and 50 percent tails.

Monte Carlo analysis works much the same way. Except it is doing a lot more than flipping a coin 1,000 times, which is why a computer program is the only way to predict the outcomes. If the outcome of 1,000 possible retirement scenarios resulted in an 80 percent chance of success, you may be perfectly content. If not, you now have a basis to make changes to your retirement spending plan.

Like all other planning tools, this analysis cannot predict the future but provides a foundation for your planning.

3) **Present Value:** Here again is a method that would be best suited for the computer to figure. In simplest terms you determine the present value of all of your resources and the present value of all of your expenses from now until age (?)...I typically use age 95 or 100. Subtract the expenses from the resources and if the number is positive then you are in good shape.

I am a firm believer that there is no one test that will alleviate all of your questions or concerns. If you run your retirement lifestyle through all three tests and you pass all of them I believe you should sleep well at night. From this point, you can begin to maximize your estate plan for your heirs, add new expenses for yourself or enhance your own lifestyle.

After you have determined any new costs or desired increases to your spending run the new figures through all three tests again. This will help to ensure that you stay within a comfortable level of spending.

This testing has exposed both those that are spending too much and those that have enough but did not realize that they could afford to spend more. After this type of testing each person would be able to make adjustments to their lifestyle.

7

Write It Down

After you have found your advisors, established your investment strategy and tested it, the best advice I can give you is to write it down.

A written investment policy statement will help you and your advisor to stay on track. What are your risk tolerances? What are your liquidity needs? What percentage of equities and fixed income should the portfolio have at all times? In what asset classes are you willing to invest? All of these answers and more should be documented. When the stock market gets bumpy you will want this guide to remind you of the course you chose. Don't let short-term market fluctuations, even large ones, move you from your long-term plan.

Through the years I have seen an investment philosophy that investors "feel" spreads their risk out by using several different advisors. Here's my take…you may be doing more harm than good. Each advisor pitted against the others without knowing what the others are doing could put you in a position of less diversification than intended. Utilizing one advisor following a written investment policy statement would ensure minimal duplication and overlap in your portfolio management. In order to increase diversification have your advisor add management styles or new asset classes. Don't add other advisors.

8

Put Everything In Plain English

In your personal and family financial planning process, be sure that your intentions are clearly delineated. Your planning documents should be written and/or explained in plain English. You should be able to answer these three key questions:

1) What percentage of your estate is going where – for example:

   - Settlement costs (taxes, fees, probate)

   - Family

   - Charity

   Hint: If you don't know the specific answer, with certainty, it likely won't be allocated the way you want it to be. Simplify it!

2) How confident are you that you'll have the money you need to sustain your current lifestyle through age "X"?

   Hint: If you can't say with a greater than 80 percent certainty that you'll be okay, then you need to...Simplify It!

3) Has your planning been modeled, flowcharted, and explained in a visual format and in plain English?

   Hint: Remember the learning styles? A picture is worth a thousand words. Simplify it!

SECTION II:
Your Family
Business

*A source of influence,
impact and income*

"In a family business, it's the third generation that presents the big problems. The first generation founds the company and has the drive and the dedication to move it forward. The second generation rides that wave. The third generation wants to do their own thing. They've seen Broadway; they've had all the advantages."

— Gale Petronis

"Given the complexity and paradox of the family business environment, how is it that some firms manage to survive beyond centuries? Family businesses are under threat from both sides, family as well as business."

— Rajesh Jain

"A man (or woman) should never neglect their family for business."

—Walt Disney

"If you want children to keep their feet on the ground, put some responsibility on their shoulders."

— Abigail Van Buren

"I want to give my kids just enough so that they would feel that they could do anything, but not so much that they would feel like doing nothing."

—Warren Buffet

9

Involve Your Children Early

One family business that I know was determined that the company his parents built would not destroy their children's lives by giving them a too-easy way to make a living. They also didn't want to ever have to put the business into the hands of a third generation that didn't want it and didn't know how to care for it.

What did they do differently? They talked to the children about it. They talked to them about the differences between "*Rich Dad's and Poor Dads*". They talked about the books and knowledge they had acquired. Sitting around the dinner table, those conversations were so different than most dinner discussions.

As soon as they were 16 years old, the children listened in on board of directors meetings. They were paid for it, a fair wage for real work. They had to be able to understand the basics of what was going on, and by 18 years of age they were all giving input.

All the kids are in their 20s now. They all have decent careers and are getting married. None of them are working in the business. Their parents won't let them come to work for them. Their father told them: "You have to go out and be successful on your own." Someday, one of them may come back and join the business because they want it, but that's what will have to happen. He says: "You have to have the ability and desire to run the company, I'm not going to give it to you."

The key decision was the conversations, the higher level thinking to which he introduced them to when they were young.

10

Determine Whether You Are A *Business-Focused* Family Business Or A *Family-Focused* Family Business

This is a critical decision – and the long-term success of your family wealth and family business depends on it.

In a *family-focused* family business, decisions are made based on the needs of different family members. They are typically based on emotion and the impact on the business is not considered fully. However, in a **business-focused** family business, the needs of the business are the primary concern.

For example, in a *family-focused* family business, James asks for and gets a raise because he is going through a divorce and needs the extra income to pay child support and alimony. In a business-focused family business, James could only increase his income by contributing more to the company, taking on new responsibilities in order to earn the raise. His needs are not ignored, but the needs of the business come first.

In a 2007 study by Prince and Asscociates, business-focused family businesses were valued much higher overall than family-focused family businesses. Another item to note was almost 50 percent more of the business-focused family businesses had a succession plan in place.

11

Recognize When A Family Member Is In A Position That Doesn't Fit

What if a family member is part of the business but just isn't a good fit, or worse, they are the poison pill within the company? What if one child is running the company, receiving a substantial (but fair) salary, and your other children are both teachers? Who should get what when it comes to your estate?

It can be both a blessing and a curse, and it may be both in the same day. First off, slow down! One thing I have found is that the "story in your head" is often much worse than the reality of the situation. Talk to those involved about the idea of collaborating to find the answers. You may need the help of an adviser that has been through similar situations. The right family business coach can save you time, money, and most importantly your relationships.

It is always best to collaborate as a family to develop a set of rules and guidelines for as many of these situations as possible prior to an emergency. You can't buy life insurance the day after you die, right? It'll take time, effort and communication to create answers for these questions but it'll be worth it.

12

Clearly Assign Roles And Responsibilities

Mom and Dad started the business. Now you and your three siblings run it together…and smoothly. You each have your "expertise", you're each paid exactly the same, and no one has ever *complained*. As your children mature they ALL want to come and work in the family business. Oh Joy!

The big question is has the business grown to the point that it can support all of the families? You and your siblings grew up around the business. There was a natural succession and mom and dad gifted everything to you equally and it worked out. Are you going to step on that landmine? The odds of that working out were a million to one and you already did it.

Are you willing to roll the dice again? It is time to get the playbook out and start writing down the rules and responsibilities for family members in the business. It's time to save the next generation from becoming the next Hatfields and McCoys. It's time we worked on the business and not just in the business.

All too often family members are given roles and the assumption is that they know what is expected of them. Remember what happens when we assume?

When it comes to the family business, make sure that you have everyone's roles and responsibilities written down. This includes your family board of directors, business board of directors, family foundation members, beneficiaries of family trusts, trustees of family trusts, mentors, protégés, business managers, etc.

Make sure everyone understands – and agrees to – what is expected of them and what is expected of other family members. This will be different for every family but the time and effort that it takes to discuss expectations will pay huge dividends in the future.

13

Build The Right Communications

Whether you have three or 3,000 employees, your most important tasks are to create a vision that others will follow and then to keep everyone in your organization aligned with that vision. I have yet to find a better way to achieve this goal than by following John D. Rockefeller's example. Verne Harnish, author of *Mastering the Rockefeller Habits*, does a masterful job at breaking down exactly how Rockefeller was able to succinctly communicate with his managers. Mr. Harnish also has developed numerous tools that can be downloaded for free from www.gazelles.com.

The key for Rockefeller was his communication rhythm. He never missed a scheduled meeting, he had lunch with his team daily, and everyone knew what to report on during those sessions. It wasn't just what to communicate but also how to communicate it.

When you integrate the right communication systems into your organization it will take you to a completely different level. Since many businesses do not utilize standard systems, processes or procedures, everything is done on the fly and reinvented, often daily. This leaves room for many mistakes. In its simplest form, a communication system may just be a checklist. Who uses a checklist? Some of the world's most successful people such as astronauts, pilots and doctors use checklists so that they don't miss things.

What impact would it have on your business if your staff's mistakes were cut by 25 percent?

14

Choose The Next Leader

I have been told that leaders are born not developed. I disagree. Although there are many natural leaders, I believe there are those who become leaders because their passion and vision were too big to be contained.

So, how do you choose your next CEO, president or owner? You help uncover their passions by exposing them to more of what they already love. Once they figure out what inspires them with passion, they'll do the rest. They'll begin to create new visions and they'll begin to inspire others. They'll even stir up an excitement that you haven't felt for quite some time.

You may find this within your family, or you may not. The key is the passion. Do they have a passion for what the business would ask of them? Realistically, that goes for any position within the company. I test that passion to ensure there is a "right fit" for every job in our firm prior to an offer being made, even for part-time employment. By doing so we are ensuring that we have "A" players at every position. In my opinion, one "A" player is better than three "B" players.

15

Ask The Tough Question

The best question to ask any owner or new CEO of the family business is, "Who is your successor, and what are you doing to prepare them?" Unfortunately, in many cases the answer is "I don't know."

Clearly define what you need and when. Create a plan that includes time lines, skill sets, and a rating of the current skills of your family employees against an objective benchmark. Decide which positions need to be filled and who is best suited to fill them. Ask yourself who has the passion for the position.

Your business succession plan should also be written in plain English and shared with those involved before succession is necessary.

16

Find The Balance Between Generations

You need to have balance between the dreams of one generation and those of the next. Your children may have their own dreams, yet they may also feel responsible for the stewardship of your dreams. Clear communication and a deep understanding of one another's dreams, motivations and passions are critical. You may need to hire from the outside and/or create new positions to ensure that subsequent generations are as fulfilled in their careers as you have been in yours.

There is always the balance between work and family to consider when we run a family business. It's easy to bring the business home and get consumed by your work commitments. Have you ever been with the family and felt guilty that you were not working? Or at work and feeling guilty that you weren't with the family? The best solution I have found for this problem is Dan Sullivan's *Entrepreneurial Time System™ — Free Days, Focus Days and Buffer Days* (www.strategiccoach.com). Business and family are both important. It is just as important to set aside time for each separately.

SECTION III:
Your Family Values

Help each
family member
to live I³

"The bond that links your true family is not one of blood, but of respect and joy in each other's life. Rarely do members of one family grow up under the same roof."

— Richard Bach

If you enjoy what you do, you'll never work another day in your life."

— Confucius

"Left uninitiated, the youth will burn down the village."

— African proverb

"Invest three percent of your income in yourself (self-development) in order to guarantee your future."

— Brian Tracy

"Formal education will make you a living; self-education will make you a fortune."

— Jim Rohn

17

Encourage All Family Members To Live Their Dreams And Passions

Everyone is at their best when they are living in their passion or *sweet spot*. For Michael Jordan, basketball is his passion; Bill Gates loves technology; Warren Buffet's sweet spot is investing; and Sir Anthony Hopkins thrives on acting. When we tap into our uniqueness and passions, and can make a living doing those things, then it is hard not to enjoy life.

Make it a mission to help each and every member of your family fulfill their dreams and passions. There are tools, coaches and mentors that you can rely on for help. This isn't something that is taught in high school or college. It's typically left for each of us to discover how to nurture our passions on our own. Some people never figure this out, and find themselves struggling, unhappy or unfulfilled.

I had the help of an entrepreneurial coaching program and found my sweet spot to be this:

> *"Passionately energizing others to*
> *create innovative visions*
> *that inspire action."*

— Michael Palumbos

18

Allow Children To Earn Their Way

Work should not be a four-letter word for children. We may think we are helping them by making it easier than we had it, but by not allowing them the chance to develop a sense of personal responsibility we are denying them cognitive growth. In the long run we are not doing them any favors.

When I was growing up we had a wood-burning stove and Larch trees in our yard; that meant two things every fall. I would be splitting wood with my father and I would be raking up pine needles...hundreds of pounds of pine needles (Larch trees are one of the only pine trees that loose their needles each year). I didn't get rewarded for it, nor did I get paid for it. It was expected that I would help the family, and when it was done I could look at what I had accomplished with pride.

For me it also made it very clear that I needed to have a career that did not rely upon manual labor every day. I did the work and enjoyed the outdoors but knew I was not cut out for a lifetime of manual labor.

19

Be Sure Everyone Understands That It's Only Failing If You Give Up

Allow your children to fail; it is the purest form of education available. It's also a good idea to share *your* failures so your children will know that you're not perfect and that they can learn from your experiences.

This is one of many things I repeatedly emphasize to my own children. I also explain that I did not find the right mentor to work with, one that had done what I wanted to do, until much later in life. I failed repeatedly and I learned from those mistakes and I am the stronger for it. Eventually, I began to hire coaches and mentors that had done what I wanted to do…it took years off the learning curve for me.

20

Create Rites Of Passage

Youth need direction. They need support and coaching. They need a sense of responsibility.

There is more to becoming a contributing member of society than, for example, being confirmed, becoming a bar/bat mitzvah, having a Quinceañera, or even going on an Outward Bound trip.

Rites of passage have fallen to the wayside through the years, and it's my belief that we are worse off for it. As I write this, I am preparing for a *Men's Rite of Passage* for myself this fall. The hope is to learn the process and begin to incorporate rituals back into our family's traditions.

Consider establishing a rite of passage for your own family. Verne Harnish, author of *Mastering the Rockefeller Habits*, shared with me that for his family the rites of passage would be focused upon the Five Fs:

1) **Faith**

2) **Family**

3) **Friends**

4) **Fitness**

5) **Finances**

For our family, that's a great place to begin. How about yours?

Michael Palumbos

21

Gather Often

When it comes to the business of family, our lives can be so structured that there is little time left for fun. Be sure that you *make* time for it – even if you have to schedule it.

In a family with seven kids, I find myself running from event to event, errand to errand, and task to task, sometimes without really connecting. It takes a conscious effort to stop, relax and have fun – but it's always worth it.

Perhaps the best way to ensure that you are gathering and enjoying yourselves together is to do so on a regular basis. Make this time sacred – and put family above all else.

In speaking to a friend, she mentioned that this concept reminded her of Sunday dinners at her grandparents' house. Each and every week, the entire family would meet at her grandparents without fail. As the tradition faded, she was saddened that her family had lost sight of the importance of family time.

On top of all of the festive moments and gatherings, pick a day/place for the family to gather regularly and stick to it…they will come!

22

Think Love Versus Blood

Family is about *inclusion*, not exclusion. Shouldn't family wealth be the same?

Today's nuclear family looks nothing like it did 50 years ago. When making decisions about your family wealth, look at the big picture and be sure that you're including spouses, stepchildren, grandchildren, and others.

If you limit your consideration to the bloodline, this is guaranteed to create problems. You've probably drawn that conclusion already when it comes to the children of your spouse.

Daughters in-law and sons in-law should be considered part of your family, too. I can assure you that they will influence your bloodline children. Rather than fight it, embrace them and make them a part of the process. The other piece that is marvelous about this is that each new member of the family will bring fresh ideas and experiences to the family table. They add significantly to the human capital of your family.

23

Keep No Secrets

Families shouldn't have secrets. Nobody likes to talk about things that are going wrong, but healing can't begin unless you've dealt with problems. Unresolved problems will eventually divide and destroy your family, including its wealth.

I have found that when one person goes out on a limb and shares their fears, their secrets and their baggage, others will follow. My family is no exception and I have shared things with other family members in order to start the process.

For many families, working with a highly trained individual will be absolutely necessary, especially if there has been a history of family secrets. I do believe that you will find most everyone already knows 95 percent of the issues and stories. Keeping secrets allows each person to create their own version of what they believe to be the truth, and that is often worse than the actual truth. Keeping secrets can also lead to a lack of trust.

24

Master the Parent-To-Mentor Transition

Parent to coach/mentor...Coach/mentor to colleague.

They will always be your babies, but if you want your children to truly grow to their full potential, consider becoming their coach/mentor as well as their parent. As a parent we can't stand to see our children get hurt but as a coach/mentor we know they'll learn from their mistakes. Isn't it our mistakes that helped form our successes?

At some point, kids will need a mentor more than a parent – and they'll need a colleague more than a mentor. Trying to control or micromanage our grown children is not beneficial for the family, the family wealth, or the business!

More often than not there will come a time when we can't act as a mentor or coach. Help your child(ren) to connect with people that can mentor them. Let them in on who you trust and why!

25

Retell The Stories Of Your Family

Your family's stories contain the knowledge and values of your ancestors: they capture the history so that future generations can understand their roots. Only then will they learn from the failures and successes of past generations.

In the past, information was shared verbally through stories passed on from generation to generation. Elders were revered for their knowledge, but families today rarely know their own histories.

Start today! Set aside some time to retell the stories. How did we get here? Where did we come from? What struggles did we encounter? What did we learn through the years? What did we observe? When did we fail and why? What was the secret to our success?

Take it a step further and write things down. I created a leather bound binder (*The Palumbos Family Story*) that has a family tree enclosed and a tab for each family member. The idea is to capture those stories that are important to each member of the family. Each year during our Palumbos Family Vacation we bring the binder, books with thought provoking questions, and ask everyone to add to the family story. As the "family story" unfolds we can pass our stories, knowledge and values to future generations.

SECTION IV:
Your Family Legacy

*What impact will the
individual members of your
family, and your family as a
whole, have on the world?*

"In each family a story is playing itself out, and each family's story embodies its hope and despair."

— Auguste Napier

"What man really fears is not so much extinction, but extinction with insignificance."

— Ernest Becker, Escape from Evil

"The best time to plant a tree is 20 years ago. The second best time is now."

— Chinese Proverb

"All people have intelligence. We don't ask 'how much,' but rather 'what kind.'"

— Dr. Mary Meeker

26

Create A Family Lifestyle
And Legacy Vision Statement

A written, shared vision that is agreed upon by the entire family is extremely powerful. This section deals with how you help each individual member of the family maximize their I^3, and how the family as a whole can achieve the highest I^3 possible.

Using the I^3 framework I outlined in the introduction, sit down with your entire family to create a shared vision. What are your family's values? What is your mission? What are your goals as a family? How can you reach them together?

One family I know has created a plan that includes establishing a foundation with a third of their assets. Through the foundation, they will help their children learn about the values that they hold close.

It is very important that each generation agrees to adopt the vision as their own – or makes the changes necessary to ensure that it is carried out. This includes children, grandchildren, spouses, and cousins – everyone involved in your family.

Done right, on an inclusive basis, a vision statement will unify your family.

27

Use Seventh Generation Thinking

It takes one set of skills to create and accumulate wealth and quite another set of skills to distribute and transfer it to the next generation successfully. It is essential that you are open to change and thinking differently. Think about this maxim by the Iroquois Nation:

> "In every deliberation, we must consider the impact on the seventh generation... even if it requires having skin as thick as the bark of a pine."

Less than 7 percent of American households attain a net worth of $1 million. Those who get there thought differently than those who didn't. It stands to reason that in order to successfully pass your wealth you will have to think differently than the 70 million that fail to successfully pass their family wealth to the next generation.

One approach is to use seventh-generation thinking. This is vastly different from today's instant gratification, 4G/digital society, and the short-term results way of living and working. Often the words I hear are, "I won't be here anyway so someone else can worry about it."

What if on the other hand we reversed the thinking? How would we want things established today if our great-grandparents were the ones who accumulated the wealth in the first place? Mark Twain said, "History doesn't repeat itself, but it does rhyme." My point is to think about it this way...knowing what you know today, what do you want for yourself, your children and your grandchildren? The odds are that future generations will have similar needs and wants.

Michael Palumbos

28

Decide Whether You're Giving Them The Fish Or The Pole

Far from being a taboo subject, you should discuss how much wealth you are going to pass to your descendants and *how it will be passed*. What you do for one child could actually hurt another. Have you heard the saying, "shirt-sleeves to shirt-sleeves in three generations" (one to earn it, one to manage it and one to lose it)? What are you doing so that your family doesn't fall prey to this old adage?

Consider how you're training the next generation to deal with the wealth you are passing down. Are you teaching them how to manage and grow wealth, or are you dropping it on them all at once when you pass? One method I have found to be successful is to give your heirs a small yet significant amount of money today and sit back to watch what they do with it. Do not ask what they are going to do, do not tell them what they should do, just watch. Do the same thing in 3 years and watch again. This will provide you with insight for future decisions.

29

Harness Your Family's Social Capital

What's important to you? Which causes do you support? Which charities are important to you? These are matters that should be discussed with your family. This is a great way to pass on family values from generation to generation. To the organizations that are near and dear to your heart, your time and talents are just as important as your financial treasure. This is where you can live your mission…bringing your heirs with you when you get involved with an organization or charity. They'll learn first-hand why you feel the way you do about the causes, the people and the institutions that you hold dear.

The bottom line is that there is a portion of your wealth that you cannot keep…your social wealth. It's earmarked for income taxes or estate taxes (often times both). What many people don't know is that with proper planning you have a choice. You may direct that portion of your wealth towards the charities that you and your family support.

Some families even begin a family charity to actively support their mission. This can be done with a few simple changes to your current plan.

30

Invest In Each Other

Your family capital includes all of your assets: financial, social, human, and intellectual. Are you investing in your kids? Your grandchildren? When was the last self-development program you took? I'm talking about investing in more than the stock market or a college fund – I'm talking about development as thinkers, leaders, and "doers."

My firm has blended together several different tools to create the I³ **Self Discovery Solution**. I'd encourage your family to support each other and create a process that helps everyone to understand what is unique about them, and to ensure that they uncover and live their dreams and passions.

There are so many incredible programs available today through colleges, universities and coaching programs. There are millions of great books available in whatever format works for you and your family members. Coach John Wooden said it best, "It's what you learn after you know it all, that counts." I like to use the acronym A.B.L. – Always Be Learning.

Some of the other tools and coaching programs that I would recommend to help others with this process include:

• **The Kolbe Index**, founded by Kathy Kolbe.

- **The Uncommon Individual Foundation's Discovery Process**, founded by Dr. Richard Caruso.

- **The Strategic Coach-Unique Ability Process**, founded by Dan Sullivan.

- **Strength Finders 2.0**, co-founded by Dr. Donald O. Clifton, Tom Rath and a team of scientists at Gallup.

- **LEAP,** co-founder Dr. Bill Dorfman (the dentist from ABC television's Extreme Makeover). My 17 year old daughter, Alyssa, just came back from this program and it was a positive life-changing event for her.

- **Julie's BeYOUtiful™ Coaching Club For Girls**, founded by Julie Carrier (Success Coach on MTV's television show MADE).

- **Coaching programs by Zig Ziglar, Jack Canfield, Brian Tracy and Anthony Robbins** have all been impactful for me and my family.

- **Family Wealth Dynamics Assessment Tools**, Developed by Dean Fowler to help families improve their odds for success, quickly uncover land mines before they explode and develop a game plan for action.

For Business Owners

- **www.Gazelles.com** by Verne Harnish

- **www.dankennedy.com** by Dan Kennedy and Bill Glazer is a great resource for marketing ideas.

- **www.strategiccoach.com** by Dan Sullivan

- **www.malinchak.com** by James Malinchak

31

Hold Regular Family Meetings

Family meetings and a system of governance are critical. Use this time to define and assign roles for everyone within the family. Creating mentoring systems for future generations is of paramount importance.

This will also give you the opportunity to create an open system of communication. The meetings should start *now* – don't wait for problems to arise; they will come. You need a system in place to handle problems before they surface.

By the third generation it will be time to agree on the form of family governance. You want to know how the family will successfully and succinctly deal with issues and problems that arise from within the family unit. The further down the road the family gets the harder it is to begin, and the more complicated it will be if systems are not already in place.

For the meetings to be successful, understanding how each member of the family learns and communicates is critical. Anthony Robbins said, "To effectively communicate, we must realize that we are all different in the way we perceive the world and use this understanding as a guide to our communication with others."

The four common types of learning styles are:

1) **Kinesthetic**, characterized by body movement and physical activity; preferred by 35 percent of the population

2) **Tactual**, characterized by more subtle body and fine motor movement; preferred by 15 to 25 percent of the population

3) **Auditory**, characterized by speaking and listening; preferred by 10 to 15 percent of the population

4) **Visual**, characterized by seeing and watching; preferred by 35 to 40 percent of the population

Why, if only 10 to 15 percent of the population is auditory learners, do we typically only teach in this manner? What if the burden was on the person presenting to reach the entire family? Every presentation given to the family whether by a family member, advisor or employee should be specifically tailored to impact all of the learning styles in attendance.

Don't Wait

Keep in mind that the moment you are gone, everything becomes left to other people's interpretations. This is not one of those times when it's better to ask for forgiveness rather than ask for approval. Failure to communicate is common ground in any failed transition.

You need a strong level of trust and agreement among the generations, including spouses, when it comes to your legacy and transition plans. If you cannot bring yourself to discuss your planning with your heirs then by all means look into John A. Warnick's Purposeful Trusts (www.purposefulplanninginstitute.com) and leave a part of yourself in your planning.

Organize your thoughts, final wishes, and financial data as soon as possible. Give yourself and your family the necessary time to make thought-filled decisions, but recognize that while it may be difficult to make these changes now, it will be impossible once you are gone.

Conclusion

Many times, we see what we think is the path to success, but have we really defined success and what it looks like for our family? We've spent time accumulating and growing wealth, but have we shifted our mindset in order to focus on the distribution plan for our wealth? Unfortunately, many people spend more time on their grocery lists than planning their life goals.

What will your family legacy be? If you sit down and go through the I³ exercise today, and again five years from now, will you be happier with the second set of results? It's my profound wish that because of this book, the answer to that question will be a resounding yes.

I hope that you've taken away at least one new idea, or that you were reminded of something that you hadn't thought about recently. If you are anything like me, you may be asking yourself, "now what?" For those of you that like to take action immediately, we have several tools available to help you on our website. Be sure to visit www.MichaelPalumbos.com and download our **Family Legacy Quickstart Tools** as our gift to you.

To Your Vision!

Michael W. Palumbos

References and Recommended Reading List

1) *The Ultimate Gift* – Jim Stovall

2) *Seven Habits of Highly Effective Families* – Stephen R. Covey

3) *Thanks!: How the New Science of Gratitude Can Make You Happier* – Robert A. Emmons

4) *Mastering The Rockefeller Habits: What You Must Do to Increase the Value of Your Fast-Growth Firm* – Verne Harnish

5) *Remember the vine: a story about the value of time in growing and harvesting capital* – Samuel P. Edwards

6) *Family Wealth: Keeping It in the Family* – James E. Hughes, Jr.

7) *Family: The Compact Among Generations* – James E. Hughes, Jr.

8) *Wealth in Families* – Charles W. Collier

9) *Raising Financially Fit Kids* – Joline Godfrey

10) *The $urvival Guide for Business Families* – Gerald Le Van

11) *The Affluenza Antidote: How Wealthy Families Can Raise Grounded Children in an Age of Apathy and Entitlement* – James V. D'Amico

12) *Preparing Heirs: Five Steps to a Successful Transition of Family Wealth and Values* – Roy Williams and Vic Preisser

13) *Stewardship In Your Family Enterprise: Developing Responsible Family Leadership Across Generations* – Dennis T. Jaffe

14) *International Family Governance: A Guide for Families and Their Advisors (Avoiding Family Fights & Achieving World Peace)* – Barbara R. Hauser

15) *Think and Grow Rich* – Napoleon Hill

16) *How to Win Friends & Influence People* – Dale Carnegie

17) *Extraordinary Relationships: A New Way of Thinking About Human Interactions* – Roberta Gilbert

18) *Family Wealth Counseling: Getting to the Heart of the Matter –* E. G. "Jay" Link

19) *Unexpected Returns: Understanding Secular Stock Market Cycles –* Ed Easterling

20) *Bowen Center for the Study of the Family, Georgetown Family Center, at Georgetown University - www.thebowencenter.org*

21) *The Legacy Family –* Lee Hausner and Douglas Freeman

22) *Love, Power and Money –* Dean Fowler

23) *Stewardship in your Family Enterprise –* Dennis Jaffe

24) *Seven Habits of Highly Effective People –* Dr. Stephen Covey

www.ingramcontent.com/pod-product-compliance
Lightning Source LLC
Chambersburg PA
CBHW021214020426
42331CB00003B/347